Restoring Antique Furniture — a practical guide

Restoring Antique Furniture
— a practical guide

Richard Gethin

Bishopsgate Press Ltd.
21 New Street, London, E.C.2

PHOTOGRAPHY

All the photographs in this book were taken by Sheila Mathews. I would like to thank her for being so patient with all the problems and difficulties involved.

INSPIRATION

For many years my wife, Fara, has given me enormous encouragement and help in all my woodworking ventures, including this book, for which I am deeply grateful.

First published by Reedminster Publications Ltd. 1974
Revised edition 1980
Copyright © 1974 Reedminster Publications Ltd

Hardback ISBN 0 900873 31 0
Paperback ISBN 0 900873 32 9

All enquiries and requests relevant to this title should be sent to the publisher, Bishopsgate Press Ltd., 21 New Street, London, E.C.2.

Printed in England by Whitstable Litho Ltd., Millstrood Road, Whitstable, Kent.

Contents

Foreword

Antique furniture is often old. Old things have seen much usage and tend to show it (if they don't show it, ask for your money back — you've got a funny one). The knobs fall off and the legs go arthritic. The loose bits either get lost or stuck back the wrong way round with indestructible aeroplane glue.

Contrary to popular belief, antique dealers are not completely without human emotion. We can often be seen in a disconsolate huddle at the back of the saleroom with the occasional tear trickling down the unshaven cheek. The cynical private "punter" will ascribe this display of grief to a choice lot having been taken up to a fair price by an unscrupulous auctioneer. However, those of us in the know realise that it more likely arises from horror and despair at a particularly nasty piece of irreparable "restoration".

Experienced restorers are hard to find. If you find one he will be very diffident about adding your treasure to his pending pile, and if he does do your job your warm glow of admiration for his handiwork will be quickly dispersed by the chill induced by the size of his bill. This book will be an invaluable aid to those who wish to put their treasured pieces in order without having to sell the family jewels to pay for the repair.

A well-selected variety of jobs is followed through with each step being clearly explained and illustrated. For example, the author deals in detail with the gluing process. This will seem unnecessary only until you try it for the first time! He also gives us his colouring and polishing secrets — almost more important than the joinery quality in producing undetectable repairs.

Surfaces and joints produced by blunt tools can best be described as rustic. The reader will have no excuse for this fault — care of tools is also explained with clarity.

Richard Gethin's skills are self-taught, and some of his methods may be unorthodox. However, the happy results they have produced on many of my beloved clock cases confirm that these methods lead to a job well done.

Ashton-under-Hill   JOHN WOOLLARD

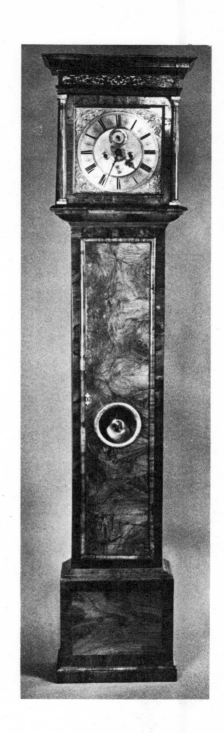

*1. One of the many beautiful
clocks which have passed
through John Woollard's hands.
It is on clocks of this type
that much of the author's
time is now spent.*

Introduction

Antique furniture is now being enjoyed and valued far more than in the past, but unfortunately a lot of it is severely damaged. It is very difficult to find anybody to carry out restoration work; also it costs a great deal, so many people are turning to the idea of doing it themselves.

Anybody who is good at general woodwork and has patience can restore his own furniture during weekends and spare evenings, and the results are a source of great satisfaction. It is for such people that this book has been written.

I started working in wood when I was about seven years old, and have always been fascinated by the material, its lovely grain, great range of colours, and the many things that can be made of it.

I began by making very simple things such as boats, then small boxes and tables; but as the years went by, I became more ambitious. When I married and had a home of my own I made furniture out of scraps of wood, and learnt how to French polish. I started to repair our better pieces of furniture, most of which were antiques which had either been given to us or we had occasionally bought cheaply because they were in poor condition.

Then I started to do the same thing for friends, and my experience of repairing gradually grew. My training as an engineer was always a great help. I read all the books on repairs, both English and American, that were available, with the result that I was swamped with information, frequently contradictory, and had to decide after much trial and error, on the simplest methods of repair that would be both satisfactory and applicable to all pieces of furniture. It would be extremely confusing to have a multitude of different kinds of stains and polishes, with dozens of colours and solvents and different processes, some easy, some difficult, some safe and some dangerous; and is it really necessary to have so many different and sometimes very complicated joints to fit pieces of wood together?

At different times I visited the repair shops of some well-known antique dealers, in order to find out all I could from the practical point of view. They were always most helpful and glad to show me round, to explain the many repair processes and how and where they obtained the various materials required.

The experience gained by these visits was completely different from the reading of books, and I found that each workshop had decided on its own methods and really worked in a very simple manner, with the minimum of materials and equipment.

There is one thing, however, that all antique restorers must be prepared to do, and that is to devote a great deal of their time to the work. It thus appears that apart from basic principles, each man, or each group of men, decides on his own methods of tackling each job. It does not seem possible to say "this is the right method, and that is the wrong method" provided that the result is good.

To my mind, there are two vitally important aspects. One is that the mechanical structure of the restored antique must be thoroughly sound. That is, it must be strong, solid, and work well. Drawers must slide smoothly and fit flush when pushed in. Hinges must work properly, and doors close without rubbing against the surrounding framework.

The second point, which most people would consider even more important, is that after repair it should look as much as possible like the original antique which has been kept in good condition and never repaired. The inference from this, of course, is that one should carry out as little repair work as possible, compatible with a sound job. And one has to aim at doing an "invisible mend". Your greatest moment will be when a friend cannot find the repair which you have made.

After some years at the job as an amateur, I settled for what I considered to be the simplest ways to work and, having retired from business, I now carry out professional antique restoration, and find these methods entirely satisfactory. However, one is always learning.

This book explains my own personal way of working, and all the jobs described have been carried out in the past few months. I think that many people who are handy with tools and have done some carpentry will find that the information in this book will enable them to carry out repairs to their own antiques and other furniture with confidence, and the smallest amount of equipment and materials. I would like to wish all readers the best of luck, and enjoyment, with all the repairs they undertake.

Rosewood Box

This box, about twelve inches long, was made of pine and covered in thick rosewood veneer, with decorations on the top surface in mother-of-pearl.

Damage

A piece of veneer, about six inches long by five-eighths of an inch wide, was missing from the back and an adjoining piece along one side was loose (figure 2).

Repairs

First the veneer round the damaged part was marked out with a steel rule and a sharp point, to make the gap for repair into a simple shape bounded by straight lines (figure 3).

Then the rough edge of the veneer was cut away to the line with a one-inch chisel and a light mallet (figure 4). To ensure accuracy, the last cut, right on the line, should not have to remove more than about one-sixteenth of an inch width of veneer. The gap was then made flat and clean, using sandpaper and a chisel.

The next thing was to select a suitable piece of rosewood veneer from a supply of old pieces, and shape it with a plane, chisel and sandpaper to fit the gap very precisely, but leaving about one-sixteenth of an inch oversize on the two outer edges.

The shape of the insert was a long thin rectangle, with one end cut off at an angle of about sixty degrees so that it fitted into the prepared gap. The piece of veneer was first planed along one edge with a finely adjusted plane, to straighten it. As the veneer was quite thick, it was very easy to hold it in the left hand and the plane in the right, and work at eye level.

2. The box before repair.

3. Marking out veneer before cutting.

4. Trimming damaged edge.

2

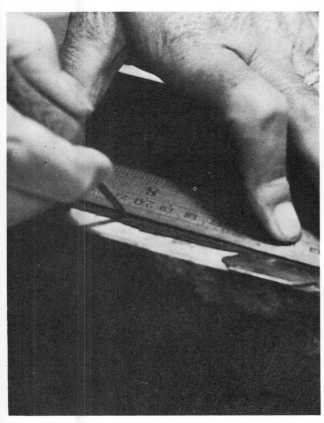

3

4

The width of veneer required was obtained by splitting along the grain with a chisel and then planing that edge.

The bevelled end was formed by putting the strip of veneer onto a piece of scrap wood and cutting with a one-inch chisel and a mallet at the estimated angle. This was then trimmed with the chisel until it fitted the gap.

5. The completed job.

Fine adjustments were carried out by rubbing down high spots with sandpaper until the insert was a perfect fit in the gap.

The loose piece of veneer at the side was then glued down, using a weight to hold it (see Chapter 15), and when this had set, the new piece was glued in, again using a heavy weight rather than clamps.

After the glue had set, the projecting edges were trimmed off with the plane and sandpaper. The surface where the old and new veneer met was rubbed down with sandpaper, finishing with flour grade, until the joint was perfectly smooth.

Part of the old veneer was rather darker than the new piece adjoining it, so several layers of brown stain with a slight addition of black were applied with a very small brush until both sides of the join matched (see Chapter 17). The whole of the back of the box was then polished with beeswax and turpentine. The finished job is shown in figure 5.

5

Octagonal Walnut Table

The base and spiral column of this table were of solid walnut, and the top was made of soft wood, and veneered with two pieces of burr walnut applied mirror fashion. The decorative moulding was made of solid walnut (figure 6).

6. The table before repair.

Damage

The veneer on the top surface of the table had bubbled up badly in several places, and was generally in poor condition (figure 7). Also a piece of the decorative moulding round the edge was missing (figure 8).

Repairs

Warm water was squeezed from a rag into the various holes and cracks in the veneer. After a couple of minutes the bubbles became soft, and the water was worked under all the loose surface by pressing up and down on the bubbles. Finally, a dry rag was placed over the surface and the water squeezed out. The object of this was to clean out any dust or dirt from under the veneer, also dampen the surfaces, which would help the subsequent flow of thin glue.

7. Poor condition of the surface.

Having prepared some very thin glue (see Chapter 15), an old hypodermic syringe, without the needle, previously warmed with hot water, was used to squirt it under the loose veneer. This was worked in and the surplus wiped off with a wet rag.

Two layers of newspaper were put over the surface, then a piece of flat board which was held down firmly with two heavy weights in the middle and four clamps at the corners.

8. Gap in the moulding.

The next morning the clamps and weights were removed, and any newspaper sticking to the surface was quickly soaked off with water and a rag.

14

6

8

7

Once the surface had dried thoroughly, it was rubbed down with sandpaper, first with fine grade and then flour. Apart from finally smoothing down the surface, this process restored the beauty of the burr walnut grain, which was previously hardly visible due to damage and fading.

The gap in the moulding was then cut back with a chisel so that the space to be filled was a simple shape bounded by straight surfaces. A piece of walnut, with the grain running the right way, was then cut and trimmed to fit exactly into the space, and the outer surface was cut down roughly, to a size just bigger than required. The new piece was then glued into place, using two heavy elastic bands to hold it (see Chapter 15).

9. The restored surface.

When the glue had set, the outer surface of the new piece of wood was gradually carved into the required shape, using chisels and round files, and finished off with sandpaper.

Then came the finishing processes. The veneer surface on the table top was rather open-grained, so a grain filler slightly darker than the wood was selected and applied to the surface, and when thoroughly dry, rubbed down with sandpaper (see Chapter 17).

The new piece of moulding was too light in colour and stood out "like a sore thumb" beside the original part, which had become blackened with age in the crevices and some other surfaces, while the outer edges and corners were much lighter.

10. The new piece of moulding.

The whole of the new piece was therefore stained brown with a small brush, and a few layers of brown and black mixture were applied in appropriate places. Fine sandpaper was used every now and again during the process, until the resulting colour was satisfactory. All the repairs were then polished with beeswax and turpentine, and the results are shown in figures 9 and 10.

9

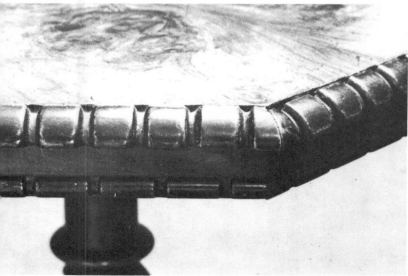

10

Upholstered Walnut Chair

This was a beautifully made solid walnut chair, very nicely shaped and well upholstered.

11. The chair before repair.

Damage

The top section of the back was broken off, with both dowels still in it (figure 11). The top of one of the side members, where the dowel fitted, was badly split and a chip of wood was missing (figure 12). The top of the other side member had a fairly large piece missing (figure 13).

12. Split top of one side member.

Repairs

First of all, the surface of the exposed break was planed down flat (figure 14), cutting off the minimum amount of wood possible. Then a suitable piece of walnut was selected to replace the missing part, and a flat surface planed on it to fit the side member. These were then glued together using a clamp (see Chapter 15).

The next day, the position of the dowel hole was carefully marked out and the correct size of hole drilled. This hole was slightly counter-sunk and the joint was fitted together. The adjoining surfaces were trimmed with a chisel until a perfect dry fit was obtained.

13. The other side member with a piece missing.

The split on the other side member was then glued together, again using a clamp (figure 15) and when the joint had set, the place where the chip of wood was missing was trimmed with a chisel to the shape of a V and a replacement piece glued into position, using a long piece of elastic wound round the joint half a dozen times.

14. The break planed flat

When this had set, the top surface of the side member was trimmed with a chisel, and a dry fit with the dowel obtained. When it was clear that both sides fitted properly at the same time, they were glued. In this case, a combination of strong

15. The split being glued.

18

11

12

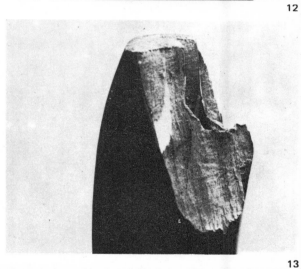

13

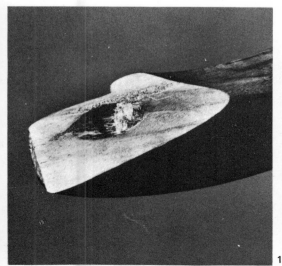

14

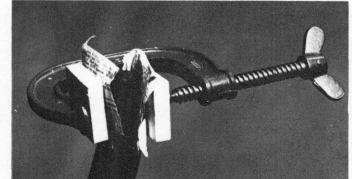

15

rubber bands (roof-rack holders) and weights were used.

When the two joints had thoroughly set, a one-inch and a half-inch chisel were used to carve the new wood so that it matched the original shape. This operation took a long time.

Then the joints were sandpapered, using fine and then flour grade, and lastly stained and polished (see Chapter 17).

The finished job is shown in figures 16, 17 and 18.

16. Finished back of the chair.

17. Repaired dowel joint with V-shaped insert (rear view).

18. Repaired dowel joint with large insert (front view).

16

17

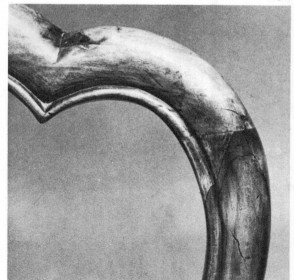

18

Small Mahogany Table

This was a very nice example of a well-made table (figure 19). The top was solid mahogany with an oval decoration of inlay in the centre. Round the sides, let into the surface, there was (from the centre) a thin line of boxwood stringing, and then a strip about three-eighths of an inch wide, made up of boxwood stringing, ebony, a quarter-inch of cross-banded satinwood, ebony, and again boxwood (figure 20). The frieze was in solid mahogany with an inlay of boxwood stringing, and so was the shelf at the bottom. The legs were nicely tapered and inlaid with two lines of boxwood on the outer surfaces.

19. The table on arrival at workshop.

Damage

Most of the joints in this table were very loose, particularly at the tops of the legs where they fitted into the frieze (horizontal cross members) (see figure 21).

Repairs

The top was completely removed from the rest of the table by taking out the screws which went vertically up through the frieze into the top. Then the shelf below was removed by taking out the screws which went upwards through some metal brackets into the wood of the shelf. There were eight joints between the legs and the frieze, and three of them were secure. The other five were prized apart taking great care not to leave any tool marks on the surrounding surfaces.

20. Details of the inlay on the surface of the table.

After this came the long job of preparing the joints for re-assembly. Unfortunately, the table had previously been repaired with resin type glue, and clamps had not been used. The result was that, in most cases, the wood surfaces had not been brought into contact, and there was a

22

19

20

gap which was filled mostly by air, and partly by blobs of resin glue up to more than one-sixteenth of an inch thick. If Scotch glue had been used, it would have been easy to melt it away with hot water, leaving a perfect surface for re-gluing. But the resin glue had to be cut away carefully with a chisel, and some of the surfaces on the legs had to be skimmed with a plane to make them flat for re-building. Each joint was carefully fitted dry and clamped up tight, and in every case one-sixteenth of an inch was cut off the end of each of the two dowels, and the dowel holes were slightly countersunk to remove any burrs, so that nothing would prevent the wood surfaces from coming into firm contact.

21. Loose leg joints.

When all the surfaces had been prepared, one joint between a leg and a short length of frieze was re-glued (see Chapter 15), the joint on the other end of the frieze being secure. A four-foot clamp was used (figure 22).

22. Clamping the leg to the frieze.

Then the other four joints were glued together, using two four-foot clamps (figure 23).

23. Clamping the remaining joints.

When the glue had set and the clamps had been removed, the parts of wood where the surface had been skimmed off with the plane were stained brown, and then the area round the joints was polished with beeswax and turpentine (see Chapter 17). The top of the table and the shelf were then screwed on again.

The loose joint in figure 21 is shown in its repaired state in figure 24.

24. The joint in figure 20 after repair.

24

21

22

secure joint →

freshly glued joint →

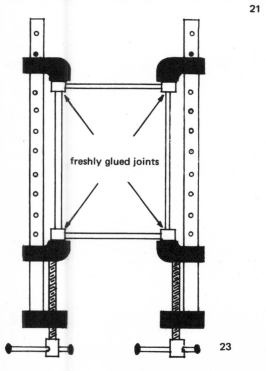

freshly glued joints

23

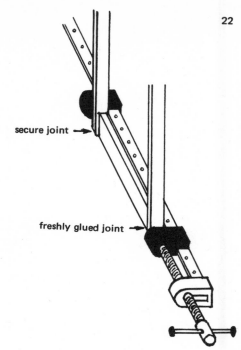

24

Windsor Chair

This chair was made of yew, elm and beech.

Damage

The seat was split in half from side to side, as shown in figure 26. The left arm was split over a length of some three inches (figure 27). The two turned arm supports were broken and split (figure 28), and five glued joints were loose.

Repairs

The two halves of the seat were completely separated; each half, of course, had a good deal of the chair attached to it. Also the two turned arm supports were removed.

The broken edges of the seat had a considerable amount of dirt and grease on them, and they were both held under a hot tap and cleaned with an old nail brush. When dry, they had clean surfaces which, fortunately, had not been damaged further. The two halves were therefore glued together (see Chapter 15) using clamps as shown in figure 29.

The two turned supports then had to be dealt with. Both were very badly smashed at the bottom, and one was split as well. The split one was glued together, and it was decided to put new bottom ends on both. They were therefore sawn off at a point about one-sixteenth of an inch below the level of the seat (figure 30), so that the new wood and the join would be hidden below the level of the seat, and the supports could be sprung into the holes in the seat.

The new bottom ends were made to fit the holes in the seat, and joined to the remainder of the supports with glue and a large·screw, as in figure 31. The various loose joints were glued at suitable moments during the re-building of the chair.

25. The chair on arrival.

26. The seat split in half.

27. End view of the split arm.

28. Split in one of the turned supports.

25

27

28

26

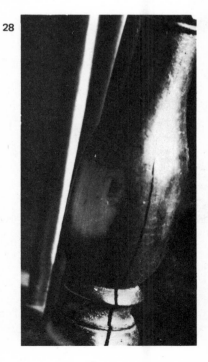

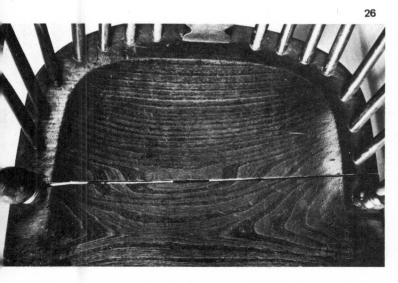

When all the glue had set and the clamps had been removed, the small cracks visible in some of the joints were filled in with stopper and a putty knife. "Brummer" stopper in medium oak colour was used.

Some hours later, when the stopper was hard, all the joints were rubbed down with sandpaper until smooth.

Lastly the repairs were coloured and polished (see Chapter 17). The finished job is shown in figures 32, 33 and 34.

32. The seat when glued together.

33. The split in the arm after gluing.

34. The split in the turned support after gluing.

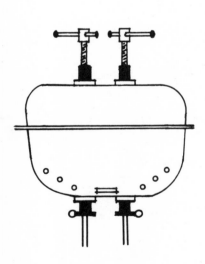

29. Clamping together the two halves of the seat.

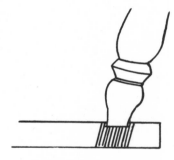

30. The damaged supports sawn off just below the surface of the seat.

31. The new ends screwed and glued in.

32

33

34

Bedside Cupboard

This was a very nice little piece, beautifully made in solid Cuban mahogany, with decorative inlay.

Damage

A kettle of boiling water had been spilt over it and ruined the polish on the top surface, the ledge round the top, the door, and below the door (figure 35).

The top was unglued and had come away in three pieces. The lower shelf had also come away and broken in two, and was supported by a few nails. About three-quarters of the boxwood stringing on the top of the door was missing (figure 36).

Repairs

All the loose pieces were removed and the door taken off its hinges. The three pieces of the top were glued together, and the two pieces of the shelf (see Chapter 15). The remaining piece of boxwood stringing was removed from the top of the door and a new piece glued in. A view of the new boxwood stringing is shown in figure 37.

The new stringing was planed and sandpapered flush with the surrounding surfaces. The cupboard now consisted of four solid parts — the top, the door, the shelf and the main frame.

The next process was to clean off all the damaged polish. The top section had at some time been covered with a thick layer of French polish which was now very rough and blistered, so paint stripper was used to remove it (see Chapter 19). The surface was still bad and had to be rubbed down with sandpaper, which exposed the open grain of the mahogany. So the grain was filled with medium mahogany grain filler (see Chapter 17).

The door and other parts were not so badly

35. The damaged cupboard on arrival at the workshop.

36. Boxwood stringing missing from the top of the door.

35

36

damaged, and they were cleaned by dipping a wad of fine wire wool in turpentine and gently rubbing the surface with a circular motion until all the stains had been removed, finishing off by rubbing with the grain. All surfaces were then cleaned with a rag dipped in turpentine.

The grain-filled surface of the top section was then rubbed down with fine wire wool. The top section, the door, and the other repaired surfaces were polished with beeswax and turpentine (see Chapter 17).

The lower shelf was then glued into place using twelve blocks of soft wood, each a quarter of an inch square and one-and-a-half inches long around the bottom edge. Three of these small blocks are seen in figure 38, which is a photograph taken from underneath the lower shelf. The top section was the last part to be glued on to the internal supporting strips. Weights were used to hold the joints together until set.

There was a certain amount of woodworm in the bottom shelf, but not enough to cause any structural weakness, so this was treated as described in Chapter 16. This treatment is normally considered to make the wood worm-proof for at least twenty years.

Lastly the door was screwed onto its hinges again. The new piece of boxwood stringing was of a lighter colour than the other, so it was given several applications of brown stain. The whole cupboard was then given a final polish over. The finished job is shown in figure 39.

37. A new piece of boxwood stringing on the top edge of the door.

38. Small wooden blocks holding the lower shelf in position.

39. The finished job.

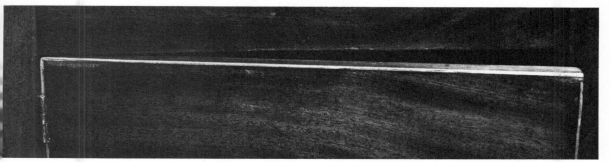

37

38

39

Mahogany Tray

This tray was about two feet long and was made from one solid piece of mahogany with an oval decoration in the centre, of very thin boxwood and mahogany veneer in a flower and torch pattern. It had brass handles at each end, and originally there had been a rim about an inch high around the outside.

Damage

The veneer of the oval decoration had lifted from the base over most of the area (figure 41). The surface was in generally bad condition and the rim was missing (figure 40).

Repairs

First the dust and dirt were washed out by running some warm water under the veneer. This was left for two or three minutes, and the softened bubbles of veneer were worked up and down to circulate the water.

A rag was then placed carefully over it to soak up the surplus water, and the tray put on one side to dry out.

Some hours later, preparations were made for gluing the veneer down (see Chapter 15) and when everything was ready an old hypodermic syringe without the needle, previously warmed with hot water, was used to squirt some very thin glue under the veneer through all of the apertures available (figure 42). The surplus was wiped away with a rag soaked in hot water, and a flat board with a couple of layers of newspaper under it was pressed down on the repair with heavy weights.

Next day, the weights, board and paper were removed, and any bits of newspaper still sticking to the tray were soaked off quickly with a wet rag.

40. Tray with lifted veneer and missing rim.

41. Enlarged view of the lifted veneer.

There were still two or three imperfections in the surface in the form of slight veneer bubbles, but these now had glue under them. Therefore the tip of an ordinary domestic iron, brought to "steam heat", was gently moved over the bubbles. Within about five seconds the glue under them melted and they flattened completely. They did not have to be held flat again, because the glue, having already dried out once, solidified as soon as the iron was removed.

Having left the glue to harden for half an hour, the whole top surface of the tray, veneer included, was carefully rubbed down with flour-grade sandpaper and then fine wire wool. The handles were removed and the groove round the edge thoroughly cleaned out for the new rim to be glued in.

Three strips of mahogany seven-eighths of an inch wide and just under one-eighth of an inch thick were cut and planed down smooth so that they would fit into the groove. Two strips were then put into water to soak overnight and become pliable. The next day they were bent round and fitted into the groove in the tray, with the ends held in clamps between strips of wood as in figure 43. They were left in this position for about twenty-four hours to dry off and set in a suitable curve.

The next job was to glue two short strips into position at the ends of the tray, projecting about an inch beyond the handles.

When these were thoroughly set, four small joining strips about an inch square were glued into position, to give the result shown in figure 44.

After this the long side strips, previously curved, were fitted into the groove and cut to the exact length required to fit between the two short end pieces. They were then glued into the groove and clamped to the four joining strips.

When the glue had set and the clamps had

42. Using a hypodermic syringe for injecting glue.

43. Bending the soaked wood.

44. End pieces of rim glued into groove.

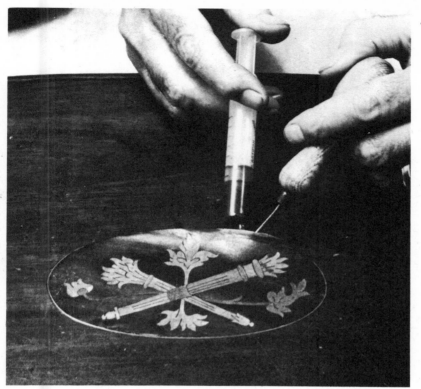

42

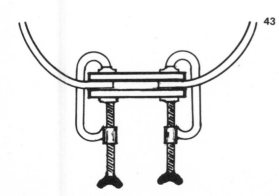

43

44

been removed, the rim was ready for sand-papering. It was then stained and polished (see Chapter 17).

The handles were then cleaned up with wire wool, polished with Brasso, and fitted into position.

45. *The finished tray.*

The whole tray was rubbed down with wire wool, to remove encrusted dirt, etc., and given a final polish with beeswax and turpentine.

The finished tray is shown in figure 45.

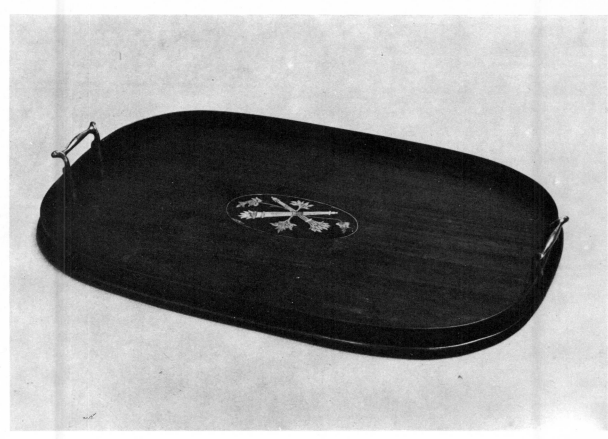

Marquetry Table

This was a folding card table, elaborately decorated with inlay all over the top surface and frieze.

Damage

There were various pieces of veneer and inlay missing from the top surface and the frieze, as indicated in figures 46 and 47.

Repairs

The various places where veneer or inlay was missing were cleaned out to remove all dirt, polish, etc., which had collected in them over the years. The surface of the carcase wood was made flat with a chisel, as shown in figure 48, and any gaps which were more or less rectangular had the sides cut back to make straight lines, so that it would be possible to make up a well-fitting replacement piece. In the case of the curved boxwood inlay the gap was cleaned out thoroughly.

When all the gaps had been prepared, some old pieces of boxwood and mahogany veneer were selected, and a piece cut to fit exactly into each gap. It naturally took considerably longer to fit the curved piece than the straight-sided pieces. The tools used were a saw, a plane, a chisel and some medium-grade sandpaper.

When all the pieces had been prepared, they were glued into position using heavy weights (see Chapter 15).

Once the glue was completely dry, all the inserts were cut down to the surrounding levels with a chisel and sandpaper.

A little grain filler was rubbed in (see Chapter 17) and then the necessary colouring and polishing carried out.

46. Frieze with missing inlay shown with arrows.

47. The table top with missing inlay shown with arrows.

48. Cleaning out the gap with a chisel.

46

47

48

Figures 49 and 50 show the finished table.

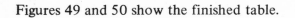

49. Frieze with repairs shown by arrows.

50. The table top with repairs shown by arrows.

49

50

Baby's Chair

This was made entirely of beech, with a detachable tray fastened into position by pegs.

Damage

The rim round the front of the tray had broken in two, as shown in figure 51.

51. Chair with broken rim.

Repairs

This was an old break which had been glued before, but had come apart again. The first thing to do, therefore, was to remove all the old glue. As this was Scotch glue there was no difficulty. Each piece in turn was held over the sink with a trickle of water from the hot tap running over it, and an old brush was used to help remove the glue after it had begun to soften. Very soon there was no trace left and the broken surfaces were absolutely clean.

52. Showing the many clamps necessary.

They were left to dry out for a few hours, and then glued together again, having first clamped the two pieces together in the dry state in order to find out exactly which clamps, blocks or weights were needed (see Chapter 15). As the rim was made of fairly thin bent wood, the broken piece had to be sprung back a little to match up with the base, and a large number of clamps were therefore necessary. An old-fashioned iron was also used, but this was only to balance the tray on the arms of the chair (figure 52).

When the glue had set and the clamps had been removed, a little sandpapering was necessary to make the line of the join absolutely smooth on each side. Then a touch of stain was applied and the chair was polished with beeswax and turpentine (see Chapter 17).

53. The chair after repair.

The finished result is illustrated in figure 53, which also shows the line of another old repair just below the left-hand end of the one now completed.

51

52

53

Drop-leaf Table

This was originally made of Cuban mahogany, but had been repaired several times with inferior wood. There were two drawers in one end, and dummies at the other (figure 54).

54. The table on arrival.

Damage

One leaf was hanging down badly because one of the hinges was bent and both had been fitted inaccurately during an earlier repair (figure 55).

The other leaf had a large chip of wood missing from the top (figure 56).

The whole of the surface was covered with scratches, ring marks, etc., and there were patches of varying colours.

55. Dropped hinge and scratched surface.

Repairs

The table was turned upside down on the bench and all the screws holding the top onto the base taken out. The hinges holding the side leaves to the centre were then removed.

The gap in the leaf was cleaned out with a chisel so that the surfaces were straight and flat, and a new piece of mahogany with the correct grain direction, was carefully selected.

56. Leaf with chip of wood missing.

This was shaped to fit exactly into the gap, and then glued in as in figure 57 (see Chapter 15). When the glue was dry, the patch was planed down level with the surface of the leaf on the three remaining sides.

The groove then had to be cut out of the patch as part of the "rule joint" which exists on all well-made drop-leaf tables (figure 58). This was done first by planing the corner off with an ordinary plane to the dotted line in figure 59, and then by using a gouge to get the curve. When the patch had been cut down almost to the depth of the existing groove, it was finished off by sanding with course, medium and then fine

57. New wood being glued in.

54

55

56

57

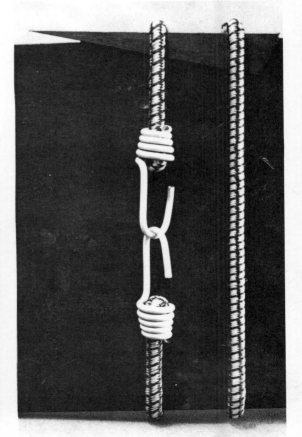

sandpaper, wrapped round a piece of dowel about three inches long and half an inch in diameter.

By the way, I find it very useful, for many jobs, to have some three- to four-inch lengths of dowel of diameters from three-sixteenths to two inches for final sanding.

The hinges were then checked over and straightened where necessary, and screwed back into their places. Two of them then had to be removed and the hinge recesses cut more deeply before they worked really well.

After this the polished surfaces were attended to. It was found that a great deal of French polish was on the centre leaf, and less on the side leaves, all covered in scratches and ring marks.

The polish was removed with paint stripper (see Chapter 19) and, when the surface had been cleaned off with turpentine and left to dry, it was rubbed down with fine sandpaper.

The whole of the top surface was then treated with grain filler (see Chapter 17) and, some eighteen hours later, rubbed down with fine wire wool.

The new patch of wood was now carefully stained to match the original mahogany as closely as possible.

When dry, all the surfaces were polished with beeswax and turpentine (see Chapter 17) which was left to harden. Then the base and top were screwed together.

The two side leaves, shown in their original state in figures 55 and 56, can be seen in their finished state in figures 60 and 61.

58. Underside of the "rule joint".

59. Method of cutting out the groove.

60. The repaired hinge and surface.

61. Leaf with new wood glued in.

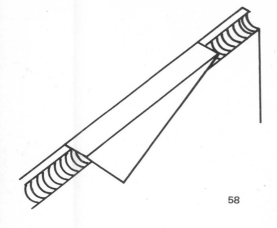

58

60

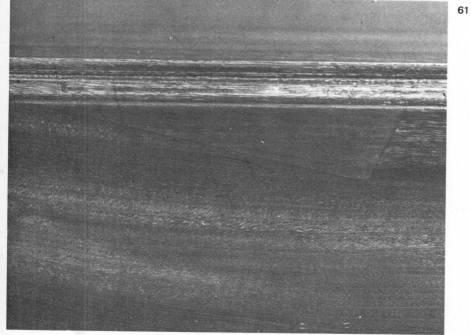

61

59

Upholstered Mahogany Chair

This was a late eighteenth century mahogany chair with a broad top rail inlaid with boxwood stringing. The spiral twist of the middle rail, which itself is curved, must have required considerable skill to make, and obviously adds to the value (figure 62).

62. General view of the chair.

Damage

As seems to be the case with so many chairs, the back legs were very loose at the joints fastening them to the side members of the seat.

Repairs

The upholstery was removed completely from the back rail of the seat, and for three or four inches along the side rails. This enabled the back section of the chair to be removed from the seat, which was an essential preliminary to cleaning up the old joints and re-gluing.

63. The mortice joints on the back of the chair ready for cleaning up.

The two separated parts of the chair are shown in figures 63 and 64.

The surfaces of the joints were rubbed down until completely flat with fairly coarse sand-paper, carefully avoiding the surrounding polished wood. Any remaining blobs of glue, or dirt, were removed, and the joints were fitted together dry to ensure that they did in fact fit closely.

Having made sure of this, a rehearsal was carried out with a clamping rig as in figure 65. It is essential for clamps to pull at right angles to the surfaces being glued, so pieces of wood about two inches square were arranged at the back and front of the chair for them to pull on. The two parts were again separated, and then glued together (see Chapter 15).

64. Tenons on the side rails ready for cleaning up.

When the glue had dried and the clamps had been removed, it was necessary to make and

62

63

64

fit two new reinforcement pieces across the
rear corners of the chair frame, as in figure 61.
These were made up from pine, to be a tight
fit in the existing slots in the frame. When
ready, they were glued into position, but did not
require clamping. The upholstery was refitted to
the frame, layer by layer to complete the chair.

65. *Clamping rig for gluing.*

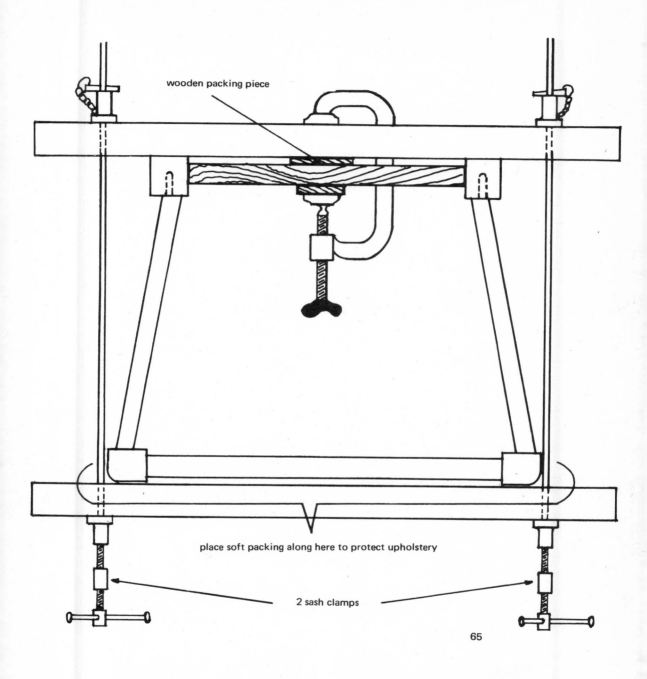

wooden packing piece

place soft packing along here to protect upholstery

2 sash clamps

Oak Bureau

This small bureau was two feet seven inches wide, and made in solid oak (figure 66). Behind the writing surface, a small drawer in the middle covered a pigeon hole in which there was a sliding false floor. When this was moved forward a secret recess was revealed below it. On each side of the door was a set of three pigeon holes and three small drawers. Below the fall front were four graduated drawers, the top being three-and-three-quarter inches deep and the bottom seven inches.

66. General view of the bureau.

Damage

Writing Top The left-hand side was covered with a terrible mess of various solidified liquids about one-eighth of an inch thick, also the wood was split where the hinge screws entered (figure 67).

Inside Top The small door in the centre had some wood broken away where the lower hinge should have been fixed. The shelves and vertical separators on the right-hand side had all come away. Most of one drawer was missing, also one separator (figure 68).

67. Original state of the surface and split wood.

Fall Front The left-hand and right-hand bottom corners, where the hinges were fitted, had been ruined because large holes for the screws had been made right through from the inside, breaking away some of the wood on the outer surface. The wood was also badly split across the hinge holes on the right (figure 69).

Lower Drawers All the eight runner strips on the bottom of the four drawers were very badly worn, to the extent of being non-existent in some places (figure 70). The round wooden handles also had to be replaced by some of the brass swan-neck type.

68. State of the drawers and shelves.

Carcase Deep grooves were worn by the drawer runners in the drawer supports (figure 71).

54

66

67

68

Base This consisted of various pieces of wood attached in odd places with large visible screws. A whole new base was required (see again figure 66).

Repairs

Writing Top The split at the left-hand hinge was glued and then the solidified mess on the surface was carefully removed with a chisel and mallet, and finally with sandpaper. This was quite a long job, as great care had to be taken not to cut the wood with the chisel.

Inside Top The small door in the centre was removed from its hinges and taken to the bench. There a rectangle was marked round the damaged area with a sharp point and a square. This rectangle was then cut out with a chisel and mallet to a depth of one-eighth of an inch.

A piece of oak with suitable grain was cut to fit precisely into the rectangle, with about one-sixteenth of an inch projecting on each of the free sides (figure 72). This was glued into place (see Chapter 15) and, when the glue had set, the two exposed surfaces were planed down to the level of the surrounding wood and smoothed with fine sandpaper (figure 73).

The bent lower hinge was removed and straightened, and the door and hinges reassembled. The door was then removed again for the patch to be stained and polished later on.

The existing shelves and separators were glued back into place and a new separator was made up from a suitable piece of oak. This was sandpapered smooth and glued into position.

Next it was necessary to make another small drawer to replace the missing one. The only two remaining pieces of the old drawer were too damaged to use again, so they were thrown out and a complete new drawer made. The original drawers had lapped dovetail joints between the

69. Ruined surface of the fall front, also showing split.

70. Drawer runners worn right away except at the front.

71. The grooves worn by the drawer runners.

72. Insert glued in at the door hinge position.

69

70

71

72

front and sides, as in figure 74. These are first-class joints, and nothing is seen from the front, but they would have taken many hours to repeat. So, in accordance with the policy outlined in the Introduction of doing repair jobs as simply as possible, a different type of joint was used. This was the simple lap joint, which also shows nothing at the front, and should last indefinitely. Figure 75 shows how the drawer was made viewed from above. The bottom was let into a groove cut in the lower edges of the sides and front, as in the original drawer.

A view of the lap joint is shown in figure 76, and a cross section of the drawer in figure 77. All these grooves were cut on the circular saw, but could easily have been done with a rebating plane.

After assembly in the dry state they were glued together, and the finished drawer is shown in figure 78.

Although the lap joint is perfectly satis-factory, if you can devote the time to making lapped dovetail joints, these would of course be even better.

Fall Front The two hinges were removed, and the fall front put on the bench. The split in the wood through the right-hand hinge position was cleaned out and glued back, using two big sash clamps. When the glue had set, a rectangle was marked out round the damaged wood at each hinge position, and then chiselled out to a depth of one-eighth of an inch (figure 79). Two pieces of oak were cut to fit exactly, but projecting a little above the surface and beyond the lower edge. They were then glued into position using one clamp on each (figure 80). Later, these inserts were planed down to the level of the surrounding surfaces, and sanded with fine sandpaper.

Lower Drawers and Carcase The old runner strips were left in position and new ones made the same size and thickness as the originals. These were glued onto the base of the drawer,

73. The finished insert at the door hinge position.

74. A lapped dovetail joint.

75. Plan of the drawer with simple lap joint.

76. View of a simple lap joint.

77. Cross section of the drawer showing how the bottom is fitted in.

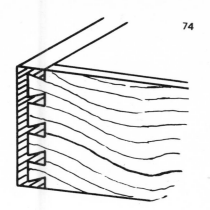

74

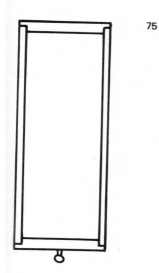

75

73

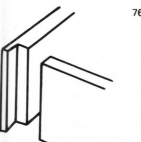

76

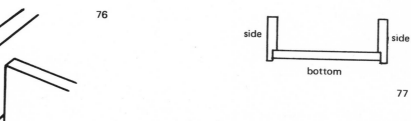

side   side

bottom

77

just inside and up against the originals (figure 81). The method used to hold the strips in position while the glue dried was to put the drawer on the floor and place a row of heavy weights inside the drawer immediately above the strips. Putting the runners in a new position also solved the problem of the grooves worn in the drawer supports, as the new runners had unworn surfaces to run on.

Some bureaux and chests of drawers do not have a complete table-top-like surface for the drawers to run on, but have strips of wood secured to the sides of the carcase instead. There is no difference in the drawer runners.

To repair the runners in a piece of furniture made in this way, I suggest the following procedure.

Remove the runners from the drawers with a chisel and mallet, and smooth the exposed wood with a plane. Then glue on new runners of the same size as the originals.

The runners fitted to the carcase will probably have been glued and nailed on, and can usually be loosened by giving them a sharp tap downwards with a mallet or hammer and then prizing them off. The exposed surface will almost certainly have to be cleaned up a bit, and then new runners, slightly thicker than required, should be screwed into place.

Try the fit of the drawer, which should be too tight. You can then remove the carcase runners, plane them down a bit and re-fit until you are satisfied. The screw fitting enables you to do this as many times as you like.

You must be sure, however, that the runners keep the drawer high enough to give a small clearance (perhaps twenty-thousandths of an inch) above any veneer or mouldings which it may otherwise tend to knock off the front of the carcase, when being pulled out.

Lubrication of Drawers Here is a tip for making drawers slide in and out more easily.

78. The new drawer made with a simple lap joint.

79. A rectangle cut out around the damaged area on the right-hand side of the fall front.

80. An oak insert glued into the left-hand side of the fall front.

81. The new runner strip glued onto the base of the drawer.

79

78

80

81

Just give both sliding surfaces a polish with beeswax and turpentine (see Chapter 17). One coating of polish is enough, and will reduce the friction by half.

To test this method, I prepared two identical pairs of wooden blocks, each pair consisting of a big and a small block. These were planed and sandpapered until thoroughly smooth. One pair was also polished with beeswax and turpentine.

The bigger blocks were placed on the bench with the smaller ones on top of them, and a four-pound weight put on each. A piece of string attached to each of the small blocks was pulled, via a spring balance, several times until the small block slid over the big one. The blocks were turned round to give various combinations of grain direction.

The results were very consistent: in the case of the unpolished blocks the pull was thirty-two ounces, and with the polished blocks fourteen ounces.

The fitting of the new brass handles came next. The wooden ones had been firmly glued into half-inch holes drilled in the drawer fronts, and were therefore sawn off about a quarter of an inch from the drawer surface. The remaining quarter inch was cut away with a chisel and proved to be a very easy job, although with eight handles to do, it took some time.

The exposed surfaces were sandpapered down, and then stained and polished to match the surrounding wood (see Chapter 17).

It was then found that swan-neck handles had previously been fitted, each of which required two holes in the drawer, making a total of sixteen. These had been plugged when the wooden handles were fitted.

It was a simple matter, therefore, to mark out the positions of the sixteen new holes required, and these were drilled so that the screws

82. General shape of the new base sections.

83. Plan of the base, showing forty-five degree angle of corner joints.

84. Shape of the moulding for top of base sections.

85. Method of cutting the moulding.

82

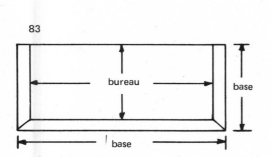

83

bureau

base

base

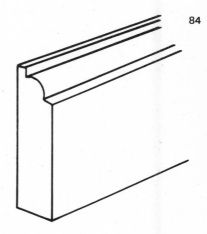

84

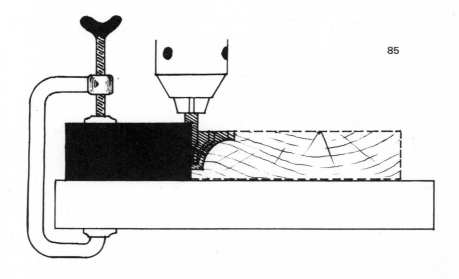

85

belonging to the handles slipped easily through.

The length of screw required varied from one hole to the next, due to the previous work on handle fitting, so each screw was cut off to the right length with a hacksaw, and the end trimmed with a file. Assembling the handles and screwing them onto the drawers was the simplest possible job.

Base First, the side pieces were removed. Of the six large and very visible screws, only two could be removed with a screwdriver, so the boards had to be sawn up and split with a chisel. The four remaining screws were removed by gripping them from the side with a pair of pliers which gave a big leverage and unscrewed them easily.

The same process had to be used for the front strip and the two large pieces of wood which ran along under each side and formed the legs.

To make the new base, pieces of oak three-quarters-of-an-inch thick by four-inches wide were obtained from an old mantlepiece, and these were shaped as in figure 82. Three pieces were made up, a long one for the front and two shorter pieces for the sides. In order to allow for the three-quarter-inch thickness of the base, the length of the pieces had to be greater than the actual dimensions of the bureau, as shown in figure 83.

One thing which could not be done with the "Essential Tools" listed in the chapter on Workshop and Tools was cutting a moulding on the top edges of the three base sections. This was done on a bench drill, using a quarter circle cutter, which can be bought for about £1.00.

The moulding required was as shown in figure 84.

The method of cutting is shown in figure 85. A block was fixed to the drill table with two clamps, to act as a guide for the pieces of wood being fed into the cutter. The guide was recessed,

86. Guide recessed for cutter.

87. Holes drilled in the carcase to fasten new base sections.

88. New base sections and reinforcement blocks fitted.

64

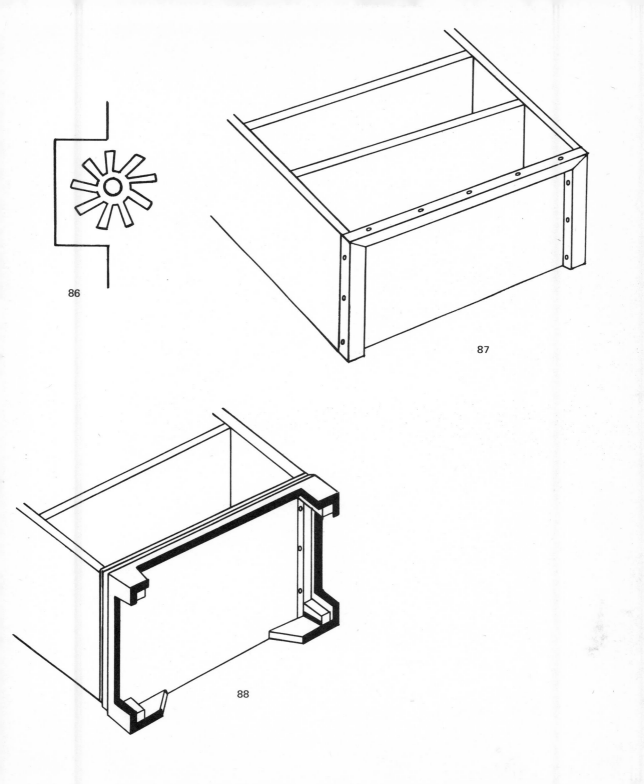

86

87

88

as shown, to accommodate the back of the cutter (figure 86).

Having prepared the three pieces for the base, the long piece was held in position, marked off for exact length and the ends cut off at forty-five degrees (see figure 83). These cuts were made on the circular saw but could, at the cost of a little more time, have been done with a hand saw. The angle could be marked off with a forty-five degree square or a celluloid protractor.

The bottom of the carcase had rough strips of wood round it for fixing the base to. Eleven holes, thirteen-sixty-fourths of an inch in diameter, were drilled in it for No. 10 two-inch screws (see figure 87). Five holes were for the front section, and three for each side section.

89. The inside repaired, including new drawer.

The front section was held in position with two clamps, and five marks were made in it by putting a screw into each of the holes in turn and tapping it with a hammer. The section was removed again, and holes of nine-sixty-fourths of an inch in diameter were drilled five-eighths of an inch deep in the three-quarter-inch thick wood from the inside, to take the screws. The front base section was then glued and screwed into position.

90. Fall front, left-hand side.

When the glue had set, the process was repeated with the two side pieces, and finally square corner reinforcements were glued and screwed into each corner (see figure 88).

The whole of the new base was then sand-papered smooth, the sharp corners and edges were rounded off slightly, and it was stained and polished. It was found necessary to put a little black stain in with the brown to match the very dark colour.

91. Fall front, right-hand side.

Views of the finished bureau can be seen in figures 89 to 92.

89

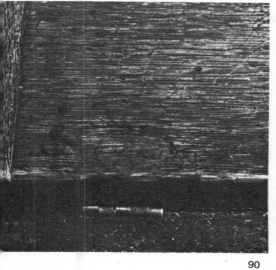

90

91

Brass Fittings

When restoring antique furniture one frequently has to replace handles, hinges, finials, or other brass items, and luckily there are many suppliers of good reproductions. However, it is often found that the surface of the reproductions do not accurately match the originals.

Reproductions normally come in either a "bright all over" or "antiqued all over" finish. But genuine antique handles are usually bright where they have been easily polished, and dark in the cracks and corners.

Therefore if your new handles come in an antiqued state, the best course of action is to rub them over with the finest wire wool, and then polish them with Brasso.

If they come in a bright state, they can be darkened by leaving them in ammonia fumes for 24 hours or so. A practical way to do this is to put them in a screw top jar in which is also placed an egg cup or similar container, which is three quarters filled with liquid ammonia. This is the ordinary kind of ammonia which you can buy from your local chemist.

Do not put the reproductions in *liquid* ammonia, because that does not work.

Having darkened all the surface, the item should now be treated as the antiqued ones above, with wire wool and Brasso.

Note however that if the bright handles arrive in a lacquered condition they should first have the lacquer removed by treatment with Nitromors, as described in Chapter 19 on paint stripping.

92. The finished bureau.

Workshop and Tools

The Workshop

This is a very important place but I have
found that, provided you have enough space
for a small bench (mine is five feet by two feet),
a few shelves and three or four square yards of
clear floor space, you can go into action. I have
set up a workshop in such places as a passage
between hall and kitchen, a corner of a large
kitchen, a dining room converted completely
to a workshop, a shed in the garden, and I now
have a room sixteen feet square with plenty of
lighting and three power points.

93 & 94. The essential tools.

You must have a vice mounted on the bench.
I use an engineer's vice which I find more
convenient, but that is just a personal idio-
syncrasy. You should choose the type you
prefer.

Apart from shelves or hooks for tools, you
will need space to keep a small stock of screws,
nails, sandpaper, wire wool, and bottles of
stains, polishes and so on.

Normally, the only real problem about setting
up a small workshop is space.

Tools

It is not necessary to have a large number of
tools in order to attain the standard of cabinet
work required for the restoration of antiques.
However, the tools you do have must be kept in
perfect condition, and frequently sharpened if
they are cutting tools.

I would say the essential tools are as follows:

    20-inch panel saw
    Tennon saw
    Chisel — 1 inch
    Chisel — ¼ inch
    Small adjustable plane — 1¾-inch blade
        (e.g. Stanley No. 3)

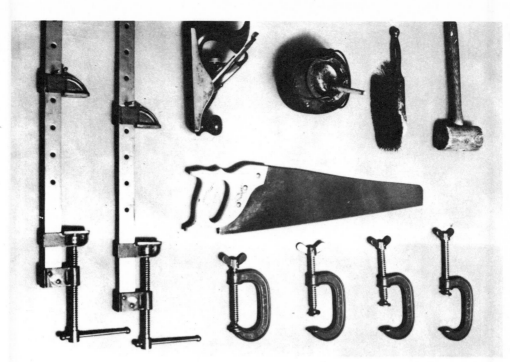

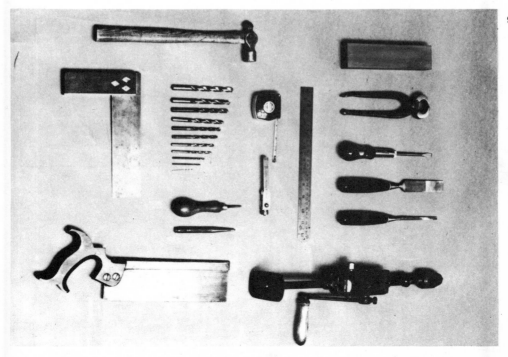

Honing gauge — Stanley No. 50 (for
   sharpening plane)
Oil stone
Hand drill
Drill bits 1/16-inch to 3/8-inch (I use
   ordinary high-speed drills for cutting
   metals as well as wood).
Screwdriver — medium size
Small hammer — about 8-ounce head
Pincers
Small punch
Flexible steel rule — 6 foot
Flat steel rule — 1 foot
Square
Bradawl
Gluepot and brush (or double-saucepan)
Clamps — four 3-inch
            two 4-foot sash
Smallest size wooden mallet
Small soft household brush
(See figures 93 and 94.)

When you begin to be more serious about
antique restoration, you will find some more
tools very useful. I would count among these
the following:

Small circular saw — about 8-inch diameter
   blade, driven by an electric motor. (This
   gives you speed and accuracy and is well
   worth while if you can possibly afford
   it.) (See figure 95.)
Small electric drill
Chisel — ½-inch
Chisel — 1/8-inch.
Celluloid protractor covering 180' degrees
Sliding bevel (adjustable square)
Screwdriver — large
Screwdriver — small
Coping saw to cut curves
Spokeshave (round-faced for smoothing
   curved and flat surfaces)
Small triangular file (for sharpening saws)
Saw set plier type

*95. Light eight-inch circular
saw.*

Maintenance

All tools should be kept scrupulously clean.
Take great care not to drop or dent any cutting
or measuring tools. If the square is dropped it
may go out of adjustment. The straight edge of
the steel rule may get a dent in it, or the blade of
the plane, or a chisel, may quite easily be chipped
or damaged. Keep all tools in a dry atmosphere
so that they do not get rusty.

Sharpening

It really does pay to keep all your tools sharp.
You will find that it cuts down the effort and
time expended over each operation and you will
achieve a far higher standard of accuracy with
sharp tools.

96. Sharpening the plane blade.

Plane blades are ground at about twenty-five
degrees, and should be sharpened, or honed, at
thirty degrees. The grinding at twenty-five
degrees means that the amount of metal you
have to remove on the oil stone when you sharpen
them is a very small fraction of what it would
otherwise be. Put some oil on a smooth oil stone,
fasten the honing gauge on to the plane blade, so
that the blade is held at an angle of thirty degrees
to the stone, and move it firmly backwards and
forwards, pressing down gently all the time.
Alternate this movement with rubbing the
blade flat on its back to stop any burr building
up on the sharp edge (figures 96 and 97). You
can test the sharpness of the blade either by
feeling it gently with your finger, or simply by
looking at the sharp edge with the light coming
towards you. You will easily be able to see the
slightest lack of sharpness as a thin shiny line or
speck on the cutting edge. Go on sharpening
until you are satisfied with the edge, and then
re-assemble the plane. Arrange for the back-
plate to be about one-sixteenth of an inch, or
less, from the cutting edge of the blade, before
screwing them together tightly.

97. Honing gauge fastened to the plane blade.

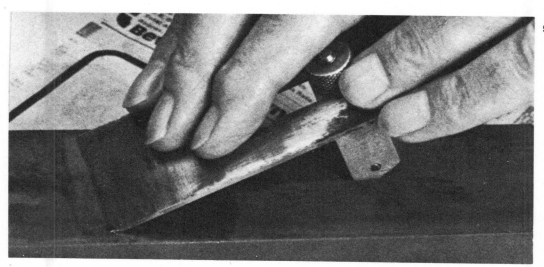

The sharpening of chisels is almost identical to sharpening plane blades, but a different honing gauge will be necessary. Alternatively, you can dispense with the gauge and estimate the honing angle.

To sharpen a saw you will need wooden clamps to hold it in the vice, and a small three-cornered file. Hold the file horizontally, at right angles to the saw blade, then move it about ten degrees away from the right angle before filing the tooth until it is sharp. While filing the front of one tooth, you will also be filing the back of the next, which helps the sharpening process. File every second tooth with the file at ten degrees to the left, and the alternate teeth with the file at ten degrees to the right, as shown in figure 98. When all the teeth are sharp, make sure that they all have the appropriate amount of set to left or right. If they are not correct, then reset them with the plier-type saw set.

Circular saw blades are sharpened in much the same way as a hand saw, but the first operation is to ensure that the tips of all the teeth project the same distance from the centre of the blade. This is done by running the saw and very gently holding an old sharpening stone up against the teeth until any projecting too far have had the tops rubbed off. Equalising the tooth projection is only necessary every third or fourth time the blade is sharpened. Clamp the blade in a holder made of plywood or other suitable boards, as shown in figure 99, put the holder in the vice, and sharpen as with a handsaw. Then if necessary, set the teeth with the plier-type saw set (figure 100).

98. File angles when sharpening saw teeth.

99. The special holder for circular saw blades.

100. Setting the teeth.

76

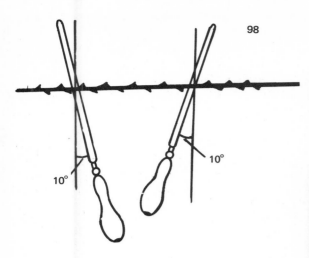

98

99

100

Woods and Veneers

Woods

Wood can be divided into two groups,
"softwoods" and "hardwoods". Softwoods
are those from coniferous trees such as fir which
stay green all the year round, whereas hardwoods
are from deciduous trees which have broad
leaves and usually lose them in the autumn.

Cheap furniture, such as kitchen tables, was
often made of softwood, but all good furniture
was made with at least a surface of hardwood.
It may have been made of solid oak, walnut,
mahogany, or other wood. It may have had a
carcase built of softwood, which was covered
in veneer of good quality wood. Or it may have
been built of oak, with a veneer of mahogany
applied. There were many variations.

English furniture was originally made of oak
which was very plentiful, good, and strong.
Then in 1660 at the Restoration of Charles II,
walnut became popular because the King
admired French furniture which was largely
made from walnut grown in France. In 1720
there was a walnut famine, and English manu-
facturers had to look around for an alternative.
They started to import Cuban mahogany, a
lovely dark wood, from the West Indies. To this
was added Honduras mahogany, which was
lighter, pinker, and not so spectacular. However,
in the early 1800's the introduction of an import
duty prevented most of the wood from the
West Indies coming into England. African woods
were then used to supplement other supplies.

Nowadays so many kinds of wood are used
that it is frequently very difficult to tell what
modern furniture is made of.

A brief description of some of the more usual
woods used in antiques is given below.

Hardwoods

Oak	The British species is the best and makes beautiful furniture, with wonderful figuring. It is heavy and hard.
Beech	A heavy British wood, with fine grain. Very hard. Good to work. Light pinkish brown. Very strong, and used for chairs, etc., which are to be painted. Badly attacked by woodworm.
Elm	Brown. Open grain with nice patterns. In plentiful supply.
Walnut	Colour varies from pale to dark brown. Used a lot in antiques, both in solid and veneer form.
Boxwood	Pale yellow. Fine grain and hard. Used for inlay and other decoration.
Apple	A fine-grained hardwood. Pinkish brown in colour.
Pear	A fine-grained hardwood. Pink in colour.
Cherry	A fine-grained hardwood with a pale brown colour.
Yew	Golden brown, streaky patterns, twisty grain, and hard. Takes a good polish. Difficult to work.
Mahogany (Cuban)	Dark brown with white flecks in the grain. Used a great deal in antiques from 1720 to 1800. Resists woodworm.
Mahogany (Honduras)	Pinker than Cuban mahogany with straighter grain. Easier to work. Resists woodworm.
Ebony	Very heavy. Dark brown to black. Very fine grain. Used mostly for decoration.

Rosewood	Very heavy. Dark purplish brown. Used mostly in veneer form.
Satinwood	A heavy wood of yellow colour, used mostly for veneers.
Softwood *Pine*	Various grades. Fine grain. Light in weight, soft, and very easy to work. Colour is yellowish pink, and darkens on exposure to the air. Excellent for making the carcase of furniture.

Veneers

These are of course simply thin sheets cut from the most decorative woods, for applying to the surfaces of furniture. The early veneers were up to one-sixteenth of an inch thick, and were saw cut from blocks of wood. Modern veneers are much thinner and are sliced with a large blade, thus wasting no wood in the form of sawdust. Sometimes they are spirally cut from the outside of the log to the centre. Very large sheets can be produced by this method, but the pattern of the grain is different and usually cannot be made to match antique veneers.

The advantages of veneer over solid wood are:

1. Far less of the valuable wood is used.
2. Beautiful patterns, with mirror reflections (halving and quartering), can be achieved.

The disadvantages are:

1. Much more work is required to make the piece of furniture.
2. The piece concerned is very much more vulnerable to damage.

Stock of Wood

It is very useful to have a small stock of wood for general use. You can obtain it by buying old broken furniture, such as tables and cupboards, which give you genuine old wood, or you can get a few boards of new oak, walnut, pine, etc., from your timber merchant, ready planed to convenient thicknesses such as three-eighths of an inch, half-an-inch and three-quarters of an inch. Remember, however, that although such wood is usually sold as thoroughly dried, you should keep it in normal household temperatures for at least three months before using it, to allow for the final shrinkage.

A small stock of veneer can be obtained in the same way. It can be removed from old bits of furniture by soaking in water for a couple of days, or bought new.

Gluing

Gluing is the best way of fastening wood together. It is stronger than nails or screws, and forms a permanent and secure joint for all kinds of furniture. There are many types, but for repairs of antiques, ordinary Scotch glue is the best for many reasons. Also it is the glue with which antiques were made. It is the easiest to apply, and is as strong as the wood that it is holding together (there is no point in it being any stronger). It can be unglued if required, and it is cheap. However, it is not suitable for outside jobs, where rain or constant dampness will melt it away.

Scotch glue is reputed to be slow in hardening, but this is only the case when it is compared to the very fast-setting types. Tests show that in normal circumstances two flat pieces of deal glued together and clamped will, if pulled apart after three hours, tear away some of the wood itself, rather than break the glued joint. However, to make quite sure the joint has set, while you are gluing the joint put a fairly thick smear of glue on a piece of scrap wood, which will normally set hard after the joint is secure. It must be realised, however, that if glue is used to fill any hollow or recess, it will take much longer to dry, and will also shrink.

The best way to buy Scotch glue is in pearl form or failing that, granular, and lastly slab form. A pound will probably not be used up for many years, and it keeps indefinitely. Pearl glue is shown in figure 101.

101. A sample of pearl glue kept in a dust-proof tin.

102. Testing for thickness of the glue.

Preparing the Glue

Pour the pearls of glue into the inner container of the glue pot until it is about one-third full. Add hot water until it is two-thirds full and leave it to soak overnight. When you want to use it, put some water in the outer pot, replace

the inner pot and bring the water to the boil. Let it simmer until the glue is thoroughly liquid and smooth. When you take the brush out of the pot, the glue should run off it in a thin stream as in figure 102. You can always add more water to make it thinner, or more pearls of glue to make it thicker. But, in any case, the evaporation of the water will gradually cause it to thicken by itself.

Never let the water in the outer container boil away. If you cannot get a proper glue pot of cast iron, then any small double saucepan or similar container will do.

103. The glue being applied to both the surfaces.

Clamping a Glued Joint

When two pieces of wood have been glued together, they must usually be held tightly until the glue is set by means of clamps, weights, elastic bands, or any suitable alternative.

When using clamps or weights, always put pads of softwood and scraps of newspaper between the piece of furniture and the metal clamp. When using elastic bands, only the newspaper is necessary.

The newspaper, preferably two thicknesses, will prevent the pad of softwood or elastic from sticking to the furniture with any glue accidentally left on the surface, and the pad will prevent the hard metal leaving any marks.

104. Clamping a simple glued joint.

Final Preparation

When a job is ready to be glued, certain preparatory work should be carried out.

1. Collect the appropriate clamps, weights, softwood pads, and scraps of newspaper, and carry out a rehearsal of the clamping while the wood is still dry. This will avoid any hitches after the glue has been applied, when it may be too late to experiment. Then unclamp and lay the clamps, etc., in convenient positions beside the job.

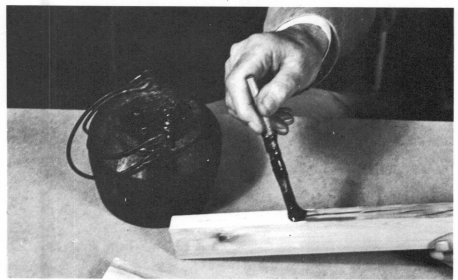

2. Get a bowl of fairly hot water, with a rag in it, ready for wiping off surplus glue.

3. Prepare the glue as explained above.

Gluing Operation

The pieces of wood to be joined should be at normal household temperatures — the warmer the better.

Take the glue pot off the stove at the last moment, so that the glue is at its hottest and brush it freely on both surfaces to be joined, doing your best to warm the surfaces with the hot glue (see figure 103).

Immediately place the two surfaces together, adjust their position exactly, and put on the clamps, as in figure 104. If you are gluing two pieces of wood edge to edge, in addition to the large clamps to press the glued edges together, you will need two small clamps to hold the surfaces dead level, as in figure 105.

Squeeze out the rag of hot water and thoroughly wipe away any surplus glue from the edges of the join. This will save you from having to cut the surplus away with a chisel or sand-paper later, with the inevitable spoiling of the surface.

When the glue is set, take off the clamps and soak off any pieces of newspaper with a wet rag.

All these preparations for gluing may seem a bit tedious when you first read about them, but when you have made them once, you will find there is nothing to it. You will also prove to yourself that by taking these precautions, the gluing operation will be much easier and more efficient.

105. The small clamps hold the surfaces level, and the large ones squeeze the glued edges together.

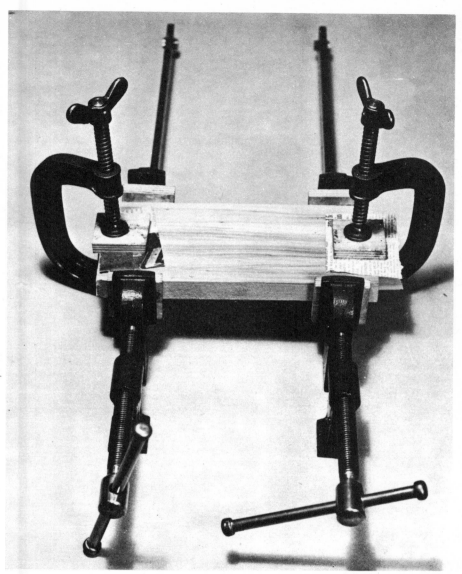

Woodworm, or Furniture Beetle

The furniture beetle, technically known as *Anobium punctatum,* causes an immense amount of damage to furniture, and if a piece is badly infested the wood will just crumble into dust.

The life cycle of the furniture beetle is as follows. The beetle, which is brown, and about one-eighth of an inch long, flies into the house and settles on a piece of furniture, where it lays forty or fifty white, pinhead-size eggs in cracks or holes in the wood. Three weeks later the eggs hatch out and the grubs start to eat their way through the wood. They remain in the wood for three or four years, which gives them plenty of time for eating, and as there are many grubs the damage is likely to be considerable.

After three or four years the grubs pupate and turn into beetles. At this stage they bore holes through the surface of the wood (the flight holes) and fly away. These holes are the evidence that a piece of wood is infested with woodworm (see figure 106). Fortunately, mahogany is immune to attack from this pest.

106. Typical woodworm-infested timber.

Treatment of Woodworm

There are various commercial products, such as Rentokil and Cuprinol, which can be bought in most ironmongers' shops, and they are extremely effective. The tins have nozzles attached, which are designed to fit into the flight holes and the procedure is to squirt a small amount of the liquid into most of the holes, and, with a rag, rub it over all surfaces which are even slightly affected. Then wipe off any surplus liquid. This action will kill off any remaining beetles, grubs or eggs, and protect the furniture for many years (figure 107).

You can then either leave the holes open, thus not changing the appearance of the furniture at

all, or fill them in. If you fill them in, use wood
stopper such as "Brummer", and work it in
with a putty knife and your fingers. Make sure
that the stopper you use is slightly darker than
the surrounding wood.

After some hours, when the stopper is
thoroughly dry, sand it down with fine-grade
paper. This will considerably lighten the colour
to a good match. It may be necessary to use a
bit of stain to get a perfect match (see Chapter 17).   *107. Treating woodworm.*

However, if any section of the wood has been
so badly affected that it no longer has the
necessary strength, it will have to be cut out
and burnt.

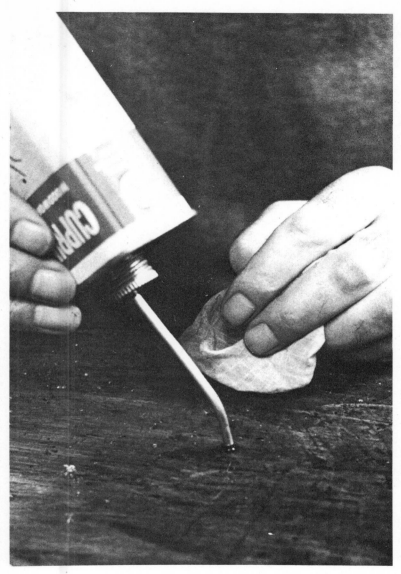

Colouring and Polishing

This is, of course, the final stage of antique restoration. It demands a very different kind of skill from that required in the actual repair work, and I always enjoy the variety provided by changing over from "engineering repair work" to "touching up a picture".

MATERIALS

Stain

There are many types of stain, but I have settled for one only, and it has never failed to do a satisfactory job on any repair I have come across.

It is aniline powder dye which is dissolved in methylated spirits, with a very little French polish to act as a binding agent. You can buy the powder dyes from a good ironmonger, a do-it-yourself shop, or a drysalter's shop.

108. The equipment used for colouring and polishing.

I suggest that you make a concentrated solution of each colour, i.e. put enough powder into the methylated spirits so that when it is thoroughly shaken up there is still some powder which settles undissolved at the bottom of the bottle. Add about one teaspoonful of French polish to half a pint of the mixture. I find old tonic water or bitter lemon bottles (large size) ideal, and the screw top prevents evaporation.

The colours I use constantly are:

> Brown — buy two or three ounces
> Green — buy half an ounce
> Red — buy half an ounce
> Black — buy half an ounce

I also occasionally use yellow and blue.

Bleach

Of the many kinds of bleach available, I use ordinary domestic "Parozone".

92

Grain Filler

I use "Brummer" wood filler in small tins, which is available in a selection of colours. Those I use most are medium walnut, medium mahogany and medium oak. They consist of a fine powder dissolved in oil, and can be thinned with turpentine. Any colours of the same brand can be mixed to give the shade required.

Polish

From the selection of polishes on the market I have settled for the old favourite beeswax and turpentine. The best way to buy it is in one-ounce blocks of beeswax. To prepare it for use put a block in a container such as an empty instant coffee jar which has a screw top, pour either genuine turpentine or turps substitute over it until it is covered, and then screw the top on and leave it for a few days until the wax is all dissolved, and the mixture has the consistency of soft butter. If you want to prepare it in a hurry, shred the wax into the turpentine and leave it in a warm place such as an airing cupboard.

109. Applying the stain with a rag. It will not go down into the bottom of the corners.

Abrasives

All you need is sandpaper, fine and flour grades, and about 00 grade wire wool, which is one of the finest. Figure 108 shows all the equipment used for smoothing, staining, filling, bleaching and polishing.

METHODS

The processes should be followed in this order:

Checking the surface
Colouring
Grain filling (not always necessary)
Polishing
Adjustments as required (at any time)

Check the Surface

The first thing is to check that all surfaces have been thoroughly smoothed down with flour grade sandpaper, so that there are no scratches visible. If any scratches are left they will show up considerably more once the stain has been applied. If you are not satisfied with the surface the smoothing process must be continued before any colouring or polishing starts. However, if you only notice some scratches after applying stain, it does not matter. Ignore the stain and carry on with the sandpaper. When you are satisfied with the surface you can begin the colouring and polishing.

110. Applying stain to the bottom of a corner with a fine brush.

Colouring

Select as a test piece, a spare scrap of wood of the same type that you are going to stain, and smooth it down.

Pour some brown stain from your stock solution into a convenient jar or bowl, and apply a thin layer of stain to the test piece with a rag. If the colour matches fairly well, apart from not being dark enough, then use the stain as it is. If the colour is too red, add a few drops of green stain. If it is too green, add a few drops of red. A touch of blue or yellow can help sometimes, and black should be added if the colour is to be very dark. It is all a matter of trial and error.

When you are reasonably satisfied with the colour (it need not be absolutely correct, as you can make adjustments later), apply the first layer of stain over the whole area.

Cover the area fast, moving the rag with a light touch (see figure 109). If there are crevices that you cannot get the rag into, use a small paint brush without too much stain on it (figure 110). The thinner the layer of stain you put on, the easier it will be not to leave lines of colour between the strokes of the rag. After a minute or so, when the surface feels dry, apply

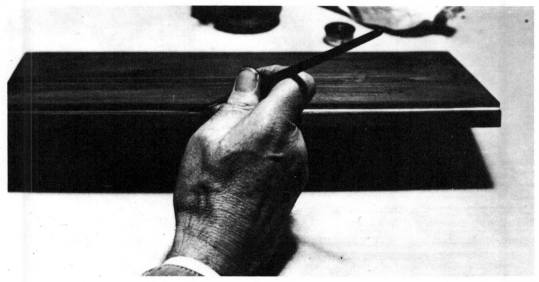

another layer, and then another, until the colour is about right.

Although your first job will take quite a lot of time, there is really nothing to worry about if things do not go quite right. If you put on too much stain and make it too dark, you can rub some off with flour-grade sandpaper. If the colour is wrong, you can keep on adjusting it.

There is one thing to bear in mind, however, which is that, due to optical effects, the colour of the stained wood may tend to become tinged with green when you put several layers on. This particularly applies to brown and red. But the moment you apply polish, in the form of beeswax and turpentine, this is corrected, and the right colour appears. Experience will enable you to allow for this temporary colour deviation. If you make a mistake the first time, you can easily remove the colour with sandpaper or wire wool and start again, so you will not spoil the antique you are repairing.

111. Smoothing off the raised grain with the wire wool.

If faded wood on a piece of furniture has been rubbed down, thus exposing the original darker colour, you will need bleach instead of stain. Apply Parozone liberally and leave it for half an hour or so. When it is dry you can repeat the process until the colour is right. Finally, wash down the area with water and leave it to dry.

When this colouring process has been completed, it is a good idea to rub the surface very lightly with fine wire wool, to smooth off any grain raised by the staining and bleaching (see figure 111).

Filling the Grain

Open-grained woods, such as oak, mahogany, walnut, and elm, will polish much better if the grain is filled first, giving a smoother surface to work on. Stir the filler thoroughly in the tin until it is in the form of an almost liquid paste. Then use a clean rag dampened in turpentine to apply

98

the filler in a circular motion all over the surface, as in figure 112. The colour chosen should be slightly darker than the wood it goes on to.

Continue rubbing the filler into the grain, and remove all surplus from the surface as this will save a lot of work later. Now put the job on one side to dry out for at least twelve hours. When dry, rub it down with flour-grade sandpaper or fine wire wool until a perfectly smooth matt finish is achieved.

112. Applying beeswax and turpentine with a circular motion.

Polishing

Take a clean rag free from fluff and dip it into the beeswax and turpentine. Apply the polish to the surface in a circular motion, rubbing it well into the grain (see figure 112). Then rub across the grain and, finally, with it. For good results you should only put on a thin layer of wax.

Leave for about five minutes to allow the turpentine to evaporate, and polish with a clean rag with the grain. This results in the surface shown in figure 113. Allow the wax to harden off for a day or two, and then repeat the process once or twice until you are satisfied with the finish.

Adjustments

Do remember that adjustments to the colour can be made at any time during the colouring and polishing process, and will do no harm. In fact, the more work you do in the finishing process the better. But do not rush it.

113. The surface after polishing with beeswax and turpentine.

Broken Legs

Tables and chairs often suffer from worm-eaten or broken legs, but their repair is usually a simple job unless the leg is a complicated shape.

An example is a table with tapered mahogany legs, one of which has been broken off half-way up as shown in figure 114.

The leg itself will look something like figure 115. Sometimes the broken halves will fit together neatly and can be glued, but this is not often the case.

The probable solution to the problem will be to saw off the broken end of the top half at a fairly narrow angle, so that there is a large surface to accept the glue (figure 116).

Then, from a suitable piece of mahogany with the grain matching as closely as possible, cut a new bottom half leg about a quarter of an inch thicker than the part you are replacing, and with a couple of inches to spare in length (figure 117).

Plane the two tapered surfaces flat. This will normally cause a very slight upward curve at the pointed end of the wood, due to its spring. This curve is very useful as it helps to press the thin end of the wood against the other half of the leg when gluing (figure 118). If you try to hold a glued tapered joint together with clamps, the two halves will simply squeeze apart to allow the clamp to close up. To hold a glued joint properly, the holding force should be applied at right angles to the surface, and then there is no tendency for the surfaces to move over each other.

The most practical way in this case is to use a couple of screws put in at right angles to the glued surface, and recessed so that a round wooden plug can later be glued in to hide the screw head (figure 119). Remember to make the plug with the grain going the same way as the surrounding wood.

114. Table with a broken leg.

115. Enlarged view of the broken leg.

116. Top part of the leg prepared for gluing.

117. New wood for the bottom part of the leg.

118. Tapered surface when planed.

119. Two halves of the leg screwed together.

102

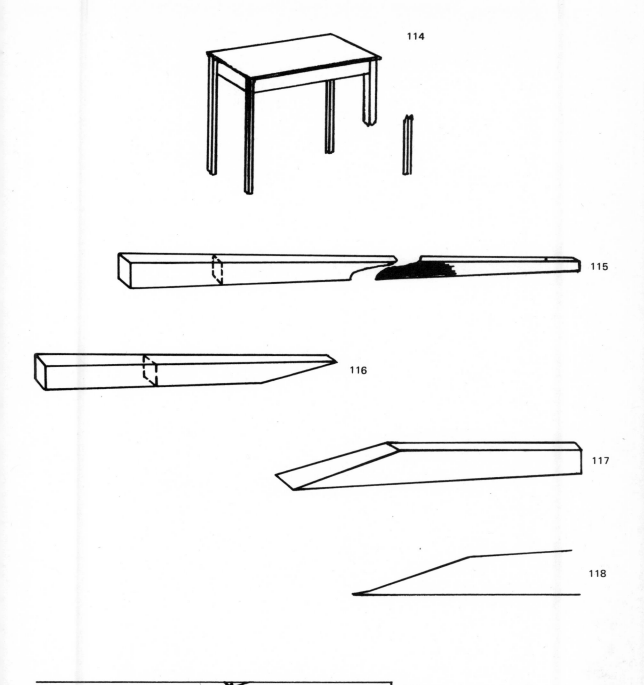

114

115

116

117

118

119

Screw the joint together dry, make any necessary adjustments, and then glue and screw the parts together.

A simple variation of this method is to use one nail to stop the bevelled surfaces from sliding over each other, and a clamp at each side. In this case there will only be one small hole to fill.

When the glue has set, the leg can be cut to the correct length and the surplus thickness planed off. After sandpapering, the leg should be stained and polished as described in Chapter 17.

Another frequent case of leg damage is a worm-eaten foot on an oak tripod table (figure 120); again, the best thing is to cut the leg off above the damaged wood at a narrow angle.

Prepare a piece of oak, with the grain running in the same direction as the old piece, and glue and screw it into place as described above (figure 121). In this case it will be necessary to prepare two templates of cardboard to show the shape of the foot. Cut the pieces of cardboard so that they fit exactly, one vertically and one horizontally, over the undamaged feet of the table (figure 122). When the glue has set, the new foot is carved with chisels, plane, spokeshave and rough files until the templates fit over it. Without these templates it is very difficult, if not impossible, to get a good match with the other feet.

Once you have sanded, coloured and polished the repair it is unlikely that anybody will notice that all three feet are not original.

120. Damaged foot on tripod table.

121. Showing the method of joining the new end.

122. Templates for shaping the new foot.

120

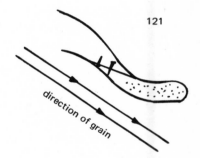

121

direction of grain

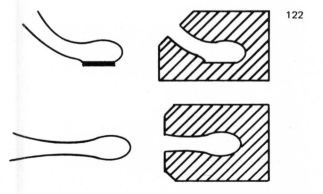

122

Paint Stripping

This is a very useful process in practically every case where you want to remove paint, varnish or polish from a wooden surface. People very often buy an old painted pine table or chest of drawers, but want to remove the paint to show the original wood. This is a very typical use for paint stripper. It is also useful for removing polish from damaged furniture so that parts of it can be re-surfaced.

Materials

There are, of course, a number of different makes of paint stripper, and they vary a lot in their effectiveness. For some years I have used "Nitromors" — the type which requires white spirit to clean it off, not the water finishing kind.

You will also need an ordinary paint brush; about one inch wide is right for normal use, but it can be of any size to suit the job.
A container such as an old mug is required to hold the stripper, and some form of scraper.

Method

This is delightfully simple. Pour a little of the liquid into the mug, and use the brush to paint it thickly over the surface to be removed (see figure 123). The paint will usually bubble up (see figure 124). You may have to wait from one to ten minutes for the paint to get soft, and then it is often so soft that it can be flicked off with the brush (see figure 125). Otherwise use a scraper (see figure 126).

It is usually necessary to repeat the process at least on certain parts of the surface where the paint is thicker, or harder.

When you are satisfied that all the paint or

123. Applying stripper to surface.

124. The paint bubbling up.

polish has been removed, wipe over the whole surface with a rag soaked in turpentine and dry it off with another rag.

When the turpentine has evaporated completely, the surface is ready for smoothing down with sandpaper.

125. Flicking the paint off with a brush.

126. Using a scraper to remove the paint.

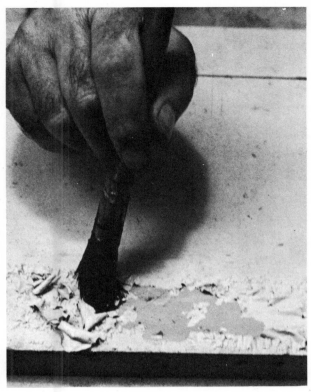

125

126

French Polishing

Sometimes a piece of furniture that has been French polished is damaged. French polishing was introduced in England in about 1815 so it may be a Victorian piece, or an antique which somebody has subsequently French polished. This has happened to me several times. In one case the cause of the damage was an electric fire which was put much too close to a chest of drawers, causing a patch about six inches by nine inches to crinkle up and lift off the surface of the wood.

It is very useful to be able to put this sort of damage right yourself, so I will give a brief description of how I deal with it.

First, the damaged polish has to be removed, and the method used depends on the cause of the damage. In the case of the burnt polish mentioned above, sandpaper did the job perfectly as the shellac in the polish had become very over-dried and brittle. Medium-grade paper removed most of it, then fine-grade was used, going slightly beyond the damage into the undamaged polish. Finally, flour-grade was used. When repolished nobody could find the patch.

In the case of polish which has been damaged by liquids being spilt and left on it, I would recommend that you first try fine wire wool, as sandpaper normally clogs badly and the surface gets badly scratched by the small lumps of polish picked up. If wire wool does not do the job, paint stripper will (see Appendix 1) and then wire wool can be used to smooth the surface down.

Next comes the re-polishing, and for this you will need:

Materials

A bottle of French polish ("Button" polish is

127. Materials for French polishing.

110

the usual colour). You can either buy a bottle of this ready for use, or buy four ounces of Shellac varnish and dissolve it in ordinary methylated spirits.

Some rags free from fluff.

A bottle of methylated spirits.

A small quantity of cotton wool.

Some fine wire wool.

Sandpaper.

These items are illustrated in figure 127.

Method

Make up a "rubber" consisting of a wad of cotton wool enclosed in a piece of rag. Open up the rag and pour enough French polish onto the cotton wool to make it come through the rag when pressed onto a flat surface.

128. French polish has been applied in circles on the left-hand half of the wood.

Now apply the polish by rubbing in small circles, along horizontal lines (in the same pattern as writing a letter) until the whole area is covered. The movement must be fast, otherwise the rubber will tend to stick to the part just treated, due to the rapid evaporation of the methylated spirits, and will leave a rough surface (see figure 128).

After waiting about five minutes for the polish to harden, repeat the dose, but vary the movement on each occasion; sometimes straight lines across the grain, sometimes circles, but always finishing with the grain. After five or six layers of polish have been applied, examine the surface for smoothness, and rub down carefully with wire wool.

Then continue the process, but with about fifty per cent polish mixed with fifty per cent methylated spirits; later with twenty-five per cent polish and seventy-five per cent methylated spirits, and even ten per cent polish and ninety per cent methylated spirits.

128

The theory is that you gradually build up a good thickness of shellac, smoothing down the surface with wire wool every now and then. As you come towards the end of the process you use very diluted polish in order to put on thinner and thinner layers, which will give you a better surface as in figure 129. If the rubber is tending to stick any any time, put one drop of linseed oil on the outside of the rubber and this will act as a very good lubricant. But this must not be done in the finishing stages, as it would make the surface dull.

When you are satisfied with the result, the polishing is finished.

If you have not done French polishing before, I strongly recommend you to try it out first on a spare piece of wood.

129. Building up the smooth surface.

Special Processes

(1) Semi-resistant Finish.

Nearly all furniture is vulnerable to marking and staining by water, alcohol, and hot utensils being placed on the surface. The marks from drinks being placed on a table are typical.

The only surfaces that I know of, which are resistant to these marks are (a) a plate glass top being mounted on a table by means of clips, or (b) a polyeurethane finish as on a lot of modern furniture, but both these surfaces detract from the appearance of any piece of old furniture.

I suggest you try the following method of finishing a new wood surface, which although not totally immune to the damage described above, is very much easier to restore to its original condition if slightly damaged.

First apply a coat of polyeurethane clear varnish with a brush in accordance with the instructions on the tin, and let it dry for at least 24 hours. Then rub it down with fine sandpaper until you have a dead flat, matt, surface. Repeat this treatment again twice. Wait another 3 or 4 hours for this surface to harden off thoroughly, and then apply a very thin layer of polyeurethane again, but this time with a clean rag instead of a brush and leave it for 24 hours.

You now have a surface with three normal coats and one thin layer of polyeurethane, which should seal the wood and prevent it being penetrated by water or alcohol. Next rub down again with fine wire wool and clean off with a rag. You will then have a matt finish which will form an excellent base for a beeswax and turpentine polish, as described in Chapter 17.

If stains or ring marks are now made on the surface of the table, they should only penetrate the wax surface, but not the polyeurethane, and it is an easy job to remove the wax in the area affected by

means of turps or white spirit, and then to re-polish
that area again.

(2)   Filling hair cracks.

When repairing a piece of furniture one often
re-glues legs, replaces missing pieces of wood or
veneer, and then finds a few hair cracks or pin-holes
in the wood which are much too small to cut into
and repair with more wood.

In these cases I use cobbler's wax, which can
easily be melted into the cracks or pin-holes with a
small semi-hot soldering iron. Wax shrinks
considerably when it cools, and a second
application may be required. When thoroughly
solidified, the surplus wax should be scraped off
with an instrument such as a normal table knife,
and then rubbed over with wire wool. The whole
area can then be polished over with beeswax and
turpentine.

Cobbler's wax can be bought in various shades
of brown, also black. Any of these colours, or a
piece of beeswax (yellow) can be melted together
in a suitable small container to give you the best
colour for the job in hand.

But remember one important fact. Cobbler's wax
is very soft, and is therefore only suitable to fill
very small cracks and crevices.

Screw Hole Sizes

Screws are used to a considerable extent in the repair of furniture, and to do a good job it is necessary to drill holes the right size for each particular screw.

Apart from length, screws have a number which represents the diameter, and when using hardwood two different sized holes are needed in addition to a countersink for the head, as illustrated in figure 130.

It is maddening to have to measure the diameter of each screw on every occasion, so a table is shown below of the sizes usually required for hardwood. If softwood is being used, the thread hole sizes should be reduced, or sometimes no thread holes at all are required.

130. The three drillings required for screws in hardwood.

Screw No.	Clearance Hole	Thread Hole
1	5/64	1/16
2	3/32	1/16
4	1/8	5/64
6	9/64	3/32
8	11/64	7/64
10	13/64	9/64
12	15/64	5/32
14	17/64	3/16

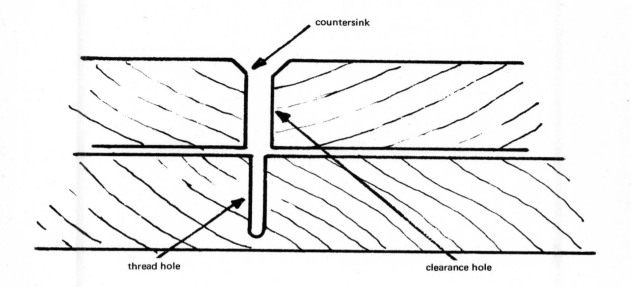

countersink

thread hole

clearance hole

130

Some Suppliers' Addresses

Sometimes it is difficult to find a supplier of various items, so I have listed below a few addresses where I have had excellent service in the supply of the items mentioned. If the addresses are a considerable distance from you, I think you will find that the firm in question will be only too glad to pack up the items required, and send them by post.

Scotch glue (pearls):
> W. H. Townshend (Cheltenham) Ltd
> The Red House
> Henrietta Street
> Cheltenham, Glos.

Spirit stains, meths, turps, beeswax, white spirit, sandpaper, wire wool, glue, grain filler, wood stopper:
> George Hull Ltd
> 28 Horse Fair
> Birmingham B1 1DF.

Veneers, Boxwood, stringing:
> J. Crispin & Sons Ltd
> 92–96 Curtain Road
> Shoreditch
> London EC2.

Brass handles, hinges, and other fittings:
> Martin and Co.
> 97 Camden Street
> Birmingham.

Tools, and wood (both hard and soft) are sold by so many dealers that it is best to get them at your local shopping centre.